OBEDIENCE

The Gateway
to God's
Goodness

Pastor Abram Cotton III

WGWPublishing.com

Copyright © Abram Cotton III. 2023

All Rights Reserved

ISBN: 979-8-9887355-4-0

Editing: Wandah Gibbs Ed. D.

Cover Design: Philipsongroup.com

Printed in the United States of America

WGW Publishing Inc.

Rochester, NY

Dedicated to...

...every purpose-driven soul that has, and continues to, struggle with Obedience but has never lost their desire to be a better servant to God.

And while servitude through Obedience can make effort feel like indescribable incompetence, this book is inspired to encourage every heart destined to experience the Goodness of God. To not only fight the good fight of faith, but to fight every battle, with the expectation of overcoming all manner of temptation and everything that tries to turn your heart against OBEDIENCE.

...This book is not just instruction for right thinking, it's right thinking for better living!

FOREWARD

The work of OBEDIENCE is our connection to Peace! Our commitment to Trust! And the fuel of our Purpose! Down through the years I've had many bouts with uncertainty, faced soul-wrenching shortcomings, and had to navigate through the inevitable obstacles that accompany unforeseen circumstances. And now, looking back on it all, I find myself saying: "If I knew then, what I know now, things would have been different!"

In all honesty however, without OBEDIENCE working in my life, things would surely be quite the same as before. Life has many ups and downs, twists and turns and every imaginable obstacle along the way! And because of these variables, we need God's all-knowing Omniscience to order our steps every day.

In addition, I've grown to understand that all the guidance in the world won't help a heart and mind that willingly accepts the advances and seductive work of spiritual **Disobedience!**

There is but one thing that counters the work of **Disobedience**, and that is the work of **Obedience**!

The work of Obedience has not only restructured my understanding, it has also given me a greater appreciation for life. It helped me develop a truly wonderful relationship with God.

My prayer is that the following pages of insight help to reposition your heart, recondition your mind, and reestablish your relationship with your Heavenly Father.

Following Jesus is not difficult when your reason for doing so, pleases the Father! Oh, what a wonder it was when I learned:

> *Obedience doesn't confine our purpose; obedience reveals God's Goodness*!

Pastor Abram Cotton III

INTRODUCTION

When I speak of **OBEDIENCE**, I like to refer to the triangular reference of: *Denying Self, Developing Godly Desires* and *Divine Devotion*. I like this three-tiered approach because it always provokes me to intentionally ponder and consider, a question Jesus asked long ago:

"And why call ye me, Lord, Lord, and do not the things which I say?"
(Luke 6:46 KJV)

It needs to be understood that if OBEDIENCE is a learned behavior, then so is DISOBEDIENCE! And so, to encourage us, and help us strive for the mastery of self-control, the Apostle Paul was inspired to write: "For by one man's Disobedience many were MADE sinners, so by the Obedience of one shall many be MADE righteous." (Romans 5:19 KJV)

This truth reveals that one act of complete and sincere **OBEDIENCE** has the power to dispense the oil of righteousness on the hearts and minds of many! And I strongly believe we need this ongoing work of obedience to operate in us, because our hearts and minds are constantly bombarded by a nation of images (also known as) our IMAGINATION!

Part I

DENYING SELF

DENYING SELF

Protecting Your Imagination

It is in our Imagination where strongholds and bondage are developed! And because our *imagination* is a *nation of images*, (by the hundreds I might add), our will to obey God, is constantly being challenged by the influences that promote disobedience.

However, we tend to downplay much of our imagination, simply because in the moment it's "just an *Image*." It is through nonchalant neglect that we fail to realize that the images enter by way of our mind but are ultimately seeking residence in our nature!

Once our nature is corrupted and infected because of neglect, obedience seems optional to us! So please be advised that the refusal to obey God is the equivalent of Demonic Cooperation! (James 4:17 KJV).

For many people "Obedience" is understood to be a system of rules that structure our impulses, our desires, and our human tendencies. But from a spiritual perspective; I view it as a thought process governed by the teachings of the Spirit of God.

These teachings' sole purpose is to protect you and I from the recklessness of our innate human compulsions, and the attacks of our external temptations.

It is through obedience, that our lives are made pleasing to God, and fulfilling to us. In addition, there is another truth that encourages my soul daily, and it is this:

When I obey God, I'm okay with God.

On the other hand, when we are disobedient, the following scripture proves true:

"And those who disobey Him, are held captive to their own lower desires!" (James 1:13-14 KJV).

When this happens, we are usually overwhelmed by circumstances and deprived of the liberty and freedom experienced through the work of obedience.

And so, in conjunction with all that's been said thus far, I pray you are beginning to see that, obedience is NOT just a system of rule that structures our propensities, but it is also the *cage* that imprisons every temptation, every act of lasciviousness and all manner of Sin!

God wants to use our Obedience as a cage that incarcerates every high thing that tries to exalt itself above Him, in you! Why? Because it is only those who live and abide in the guidance of **OBEDIENCE** that ever really experience the liberty and freedom that comes through obedience.

Because of the way our hearts work in concert with our minds, we have to pay close attention to the images around us that are constantly being introduced to our nature! Keep in mind; the more images we allow to enter in, the bigger the Nation of Images becomes!

Unbridled imagination has been known to literally corrupt the morality of men. In addition, an imagination infused with demonic influence can destroy a life, and cause the imprisonment of a soul without any remorse!

Therefore, we must protect our imagination as it is one of the ways God develops the foresight of our faith (Proverbs 4:23 KJV). Not to mention that it is through the wonderful work of our imagination that we embark upon the beauty of God's faithfulness to us.

Allow me to share this scripture with you: "After walking with Jesus for a short while, his disciples would soon learn, nothing is more crucial to your calling, than OBEDIENCE!" (Matthew 17:5-6 KJV).

Contrary to what many believe, our imagination is the canvas for our calling. I say this because, God is constantly working on this canvas, revealing every one of His promises to us on it. Which is why it is imperative that we protect our imagination from strongholds...

A stronghold is an internal compulsion that subdues our external willingness to resist sin. We must do our very best to avoid being ensnared by strongholds because of the effect they have on our successes, both naturally and spiritually. We must never lose sight of this truth; a stronghold not pulled down, is a heart and mind susceptible to demonic influence!

Ponder this; if Obedience is Better than Sacrifice (I Samuel 15:22 KJV), then it's no wonder all disobedience is subject to suffering! It's important to understand that a holy and healthy imagination is also the reservoir that holds the substance of your purpose! And this reservoir is not only beneficial for our purpose, but it is also consecrated for our potential!

NOTE: Sacrificing spiritual substance to entertain vain imaginations is just as damaging as starving your purpose and squandering your potential!

Keep in mind; your *NOW* faith, is also the *substance* of your expected hope! (Hebrews 11:1 KJV). And your expected hope is manifested through the diligent work of your obedience.

When you are careful to protect your imagination and give committed diligence to maintaining a Father-filtered faith through obedience; you can rest assured that your obedience *TO* God, will release His greatness *IN* YOU!

There are so many images that try to exalt themselves above your knowledge of God. They often appear during moments of hardship, struggle, uncertainty, etc. They present themselves as situational options but prove themselves to be the absolute worst form of spiritual opposition!

NOTE: Most Demonic influences are constantly trying to engage your imagination to embrace the illusion that there is a right way, to do wrong!

This kind of influence is not only trying to disrupt your thoughts but is also trying to destroy your will to obey God! Always remember; vain imaginations want to derail your decisions to do the right things by prompting you to consider doing the wrong things! This is why we must stay ready to bring every insubordinate thought into captivity through our obedience to the word of God.

In the spirit of transparency, let me share this with you: I remember times in my walk (my journey if you will) with God, where there were moments of immense struggle and failure.

Being a novice of God's power within me, I pinned every shortcoming on **weakness**! But as I grew in the spirit and began to examine my walk with an honest and spirit-filled heart, I saw for myself that I was not weak. I just wasn't ready to **OBEY** the spirit of God! Hence, I didn't protect my imagination from evil influences, my own lower desires and those high things that had exalted themselves above what I knew about God.

But, because of God's grace, mercy, and lovingkindness; I learned that the best way to protect my imagination, was to confine every vain thought (imagination) in the cage of my OBEDIENCE! It was then that I realized, the only way vanity can corrupt my mind, is if I disobey God!

REFLECTION

Are your thoughts more about pleasing yourself, or fulfilling your purpose?

_____
_____
_____
_____
_____
_____
_____

What do you believe God expects of you/us?

_____
_____
_____
_____
_____
_____
_____
_____
_____

How has your moral neglect hindered your spiritual ability to OBEY God?

_____
_____
_____
_____
_____
_____
_____
_____

List some things you can do to protect your relationship with God from vain imagination?

_____
_____
_____
_____
_____
_____
_____
_____

Part II

Developing Godly Desires

Developing Godly Desires

Obedience is Better Than Sacrifice

Take a moment right here and imagine being in a place free of sickness, poverty, violence, corruption, deficiency, and every other form of affliction. Is that not a soothing image? Well, Jesus endured all of life's afflictions on the cross, so we could receive all His Father's affection on Earth. When we put (I Samuel 15:22) in perspective, we begin to understand that whatever God requires of us, should be carried out to the best of our ability. Because knowing emphatically what God requires of us, but only doing what we want to do, is no less than spiritual **Rebellion** (vs.23).

I truly believe that *obedience is better than sacrifice*. I believe this because our **sacrifices** are usually a testament to our commitment to being naturally *responsible*. Whereas our **obedience** is a testament to our commitment to be spiritually *righteous*. While sacrifices can yield a sense of self-gratification, they are incomparable to the heart longing to please God more than anything or anyone else.

There are many sacrifices that can render you responsible, but it is only through obedience one can be rendered righteous unto God! Truthfully speaking, it's not a sacrifice, when you don't mind giving up what doesn't really matter to you anyway! But **We** mattered so much to God, that **He** sacrificed the best He had: His Son! And so, even God himself, was and is, obedient to His own will!

When we purpose to serve God through obedience, no matter what the sacrifice is, God is WELL pleased. My dear brothers and sisters, when our willingness to obey, becomes more important than the thought of what we're sacrificing, we are reaffirming to God what our relationship with Him really means to us. And so, we must obey our Heavenly Father, just as Jesus did. No matter what, He obeyed! (Hebrews 5:8).

In addition, as Pastor of a local church, I am constantly reminding the people of God, "You don't get BETTER without the work and willingness to do things DIFFERENTLY!" Hence, here is another reason Obedience is better than Sacrifice: **Life is really *Different*, when you obey without reservation**!

I'm not talking about an ordinary *different*! I'm talking about a supernatural and divine *different*! A different that ***comforts*** you when Obedience is **PAINFUL**! A *different* that ***guides*** you through the **PROCESS** of Obedience! And a *different* that ***encourages*** your **PERSEVERANCE** during Obedience!

The collaboration of ***Pain, Process***, and ***Perseverance*** are the building blocks God uses to perfect our Future. This dynamic trio is the set-up crew that makes it possible for you to give God the best you have to offer.

These building blocks and the trials that accompany them, have tremendous purpose! How? Because of their ability to strengthen our will to do the right thing while going forward! When God allows any of us to experience the repercussions of disobedience, it's because He wants to destroy what is influencing us to disobey and develop in us what will bring Him glory: **Obedience!**

I think this is a perfect place to inform you that it is absolutely impossible to Obey God, without having to fight with your flesh! Please don't ever lose sight of this spiritual truth. Your flesh is carnal and corrupt! It always wants what it wants! And that, people of God, **is the real reason Obedience is sometimes so seemingly painful!**

You cannot overcome the fight in your flesh, without feeling the affliction in your spirit! Therefore, be comforted in this: the most incredible aspect of being obedient unto God is:

"Though we may experience travail in the moment, we will have unspeakable joy when it's all over!" (Psalms 30:5 KJV).

As a husband and a father, I witnessed the birth of each of my children. On the flipside of that experience, I also witnessed the agony women go through in the process. After all the groaning, the anguish, and the exertion of pushing; in the end, each child brought tremendous joy to their mother.

Though I was privileged to witness each birth, I was unable to truly understand the extraordinary work a woman has to endure in order to give birth. Likewise, **OBEDIENCE** may be painful to endure, but necessary for a breakthrough!

Therefore, let your heart be encouraged. Continue to obey the will of God, so you can experience the joy of seeing your Pain become your Promotion.

Now that you've come to grips with the truth that OBEDIENCE is better than Sacrifice, and that it often travels the corridors of Pain, Process, and Perseverance: keep putting one foot in front of the other. Keep walking, keep moving forward, and you'll soon discover you're almost there!

By now you're probably starting to feel an overwhelming and unexplainable feeling of strength accompanied by a presence that is drawing you, comforting you, and speaking to you. It's like you're entering another dimension from within. And guess what? You are! Now relax and feel the very presence of God. You've arrived my friend. Your **Obedience** has ushered you to the Goodness of God.

REFLECTION

What sacrifices do you believe will help you become a better servant to God, and an obedient example to others?

_____
_____
_____
_____
_____
_____
_____

What gets in the way and challenges your will to obey God more than anything else?

_____
_____
_____
_____
_____
_____
_____

Are you truly satisfied with the sacrifices that continually leave your Spirit discontented? Write down some changes you plan to make:

_____
_____
_____
_____
_____
_____
_____
_____

Are you giving yourself the same chance to grow through OBEDIENCE that you do to grieve through disobedience?

_____
_____
_____
_____
_____
_____

Part III

DIVINE DEVOTION

DIVINE DEVOTION

The Goodness of God

King David wrote:

> "Surely *goodness* and mercy, shall follow me all the days of my life."
> (Psalms 23:6 KJV)

I believe King David was speaking from a place he had finally reached in his heart: **God's Goodness**!

David went through tremendous amounts of pain in life. He was taken from his father's house. He stood toe to toe with a Giant. He experienced bloodshed, betrayal and deception.

He fell to temptation, committed adultery, facilitated a murder, and even experienced the loss of a child! But, and through it all, the one thing that was ever-present and constant in King David's life, was the Goodness of God!

King David went on to pen...

"I had fainted, unless I had believed to see the *Goodness* of God in the land of the living."
(Psalms 27:13 KJV)

David was in essence testifying that his obedience, though sometimes more than even he thought he could bear, did not come without struggle! But glory to God, because he stayed true to Obedience, it allowed him to see and always experience what he had been promised: the Goodness of God. Therefore, throughout his life, he endured every hardship, despite the countless times he felt like giving up!

Have you ever been there in your heart? I know I have. After everything David lived through, he left us with a word of encouragement: Keep believing! Keep Obeying! Because the Goodness of God, is worth the struggle!

My dear brothers and sisters, God knows that obedience brings with it friction in the flesh. But friction in the flesh, that develops faithfulness in the soul...is proper execution of **Obedience**! In fact, Jesus had this to say about those who obeyed His Father's love: "Blessed are the pure in heart, for they shall *see* God" (Matthew 5:8 KJV).

I bet at this point you are somewhat encouraged and feeling better about life and your walk with God. However, deep within, you may still be asking yourself: **WHERE** exactly is the Goodness of God? **What** does it look like? And the answer to both these questions is resting confidently in your OBEDIENCE! You see, every time you say *NO* to temptation, bad thinking, unrighteous influences, etc. you experience the preeminent power of God's Goodness! And even though you may not have known this before now, this is your public announcement! God's Goodness **is** His Presence and His Authority...**in YOU!** This power is God on the scene! God in your struggle! and God undefeatable! This is the same Authority and Presence that raised Jesus from the dead! It is the same Authority and Presence that causes demons to tremble, and it is the same Authority and Presence that gives every **OBEDIENT** soul the ability to resist temptation and live a life filled with power and purpose!

He promised to never leave you, nor forsake you! God wants us to understand that when we accepted His son, Jesus Christ, as our Lord and Savior, His Goodness (presence) has been with us ever since! God allowed you to go through and undergo a few things to help you trust Him more. And so, contrary to your feelings or inner voice (that is the flesh), it is a blessing when God uses Obedience to reveal His Goodness; and at the same time, allows us to establish and further develop our faithfulness to Him. Remember what Jesus said: "But seek ye the kingdom of God, and all these things shall be added to you" (Luke 12:31 KJV). He continued, "for where your treasure is, there will your heart be also" (vs.34). Every heart, that obeys to make God and all His splendor their treasure...God says, "that's where you'll find my *Goodness*."

So now, I pray you can see that Obedience, like Faithfulness, like a church or a sanctuary, is an actual dwelling place for God's very essence! Again, let me remind you; wherever you find God's Goodness, you're also in His Presence! Oh, just think about it, every time we obey God, we have His presence, and with every obedient act, His promises are released!

I can imagine that at this point you're experiencing the same thing I am right now! Everything that's been revealed, just running through your veins! That's the spirit of God Himself! Not just upon you! But moving in you! And that feeling of empowerment is the reward for your Obedience. Which now gives you all the strength to do all things in Christ! (Philippians 4:13 KJV). And so here again, Jesus helps us gain a greater perspective of God's Goodness with these words, "There is none Good, but one, that is GOD" (Mark 10:18 KJV). Jesus wants us to know that, **Good**, is **God** Himself! And while He is grossly imitated by opposing minds and opinions, every opposer will find out in the end, that it is impossible to duplicate God's will, His ways, or His Preeminence! Because God is God, and God all by Himself! And beside Him, there is no other! (Isaiah 45:5 KJV).

I am confident that you can now feel all the encouragement that has been given to increase your desire to remain a faithful follower through the work of OBEDIENCE. I pray this book and all its content is a constant reminder of the importance of obeying God, no matter what!

Okay, now, before I let you go, allow me to share one last transparent moment with you:

This book was inspired when the Holy Spirit urged one of the elders, during one of our Bible studies, to tell me...You need to write a book on OBEDIENCE. It was in that very moment; I humbly accepted and **obeyed** the call to put on paper what God had already put in my heart. I prayed and humbly said, "Lord speak to me." I needed Him to speak to me, before I spoke to you. Why? Because I know that I too still have lessons in *OBEDIENCE* to learn. And so, this book is not me preaching another sermon to the masses, but rather me receiving a little more of ***God's Goodness*** myself!

Now, I too have a better understanding of what King David meant when he said: "I had rather be a doorkeeper in the house of my God, than to dwell in the tents of wickedness!" (Psalms 84:10 KJV).

King David finally understood and accepted that the Gateway to the *Goodness of God*, was the corridor of his own **OBEDIENCE**.

REFLECTION

Are you willing to let God reveal His Goodness through your OBEDIENCE? Indicate two areas you can practice OBEDIENCE:

_____
_____
_____
_____
_____

Can you see how your OBEDIENCE can establish your devotion to God? List two instances where you recently experienced increased closeness to God:

_____
_____
_____
_____
_____

At this very moment, is your heart in a better place because of what you have just learned? How so?

_____
_____
_____
_____
_____
_____
_____

Is not God's Goodness (His Authority and Presence), the best place you have ever been? List two ways you have experienced the difference:

_____
_____
_____
_____
_____
_____
_____

ABOUT THE AUTHOR

Pastor Abram Cotton III is currently Senior Pastor at King of Glory Ministries in Rochester, NY. He previously served 10 years as Assistant Pastor of Christian Love Bible Church under the leadership of Pastor Abram Cotton Jr.

Pastor Cotton III is a spiritual mentor and guide. A great encourager and teacher, he doesn't simply talk the talk; he literally walks the walk.

A naturally gifted wordsmith, he has a tremendous ability to understand the meaning and value of God's Word.

Humble and open to all, he unabashedly and frequently shares his personal testimony, thanking God all the way, thus becoming a true beacon of Christian forgiveness and obedience.

Pastor Cotton III's commitment and joy are unmistakable and his values uncompromising. Oh, and did I mention his wonderful sense of humor! Thank you, Pastor Cotton for showing us the way. ---Dr. Wandah Gibbs